London, New York, Munich, Melbourne, Delhi

Text by
Harriet Griffey
For Josh and Robbie

Project editor Jane Laing
Project art editors Christine Lacey, Glenda Fisher
Senior editor Julia North
Managing art editor Tracey Ward
Production controller Louise Daly
Photography Ruth Jenkinson
Art direction Sally Smallwood

First published in Great Britain in 2002 by
Dorling Kindersley, A Penguin Company
80 Strand, London, WC2R 0RL

A CIP catalogue record for this book is available from the
British Library

ISBN 0 7513 3719 6

Reproduced by Colourscan Overseas Pte Ltd, Singapore
Printed by Graphicom, Italy

See our complete catalogue at
www.dk.com

Contents

A message to parents from Johnson & Johnson

For more than 100 years, Johnson & Johnson has been caring for babies. Our baby products help mothers and fathers soothe, comfort, and nurture a deep, loving bond with their child through everyday care.

Building on our commitment to children and families, Johnson & Johnson established the Johnson & Johnson Pediatric Institute, LLC. This unique organization promotes continued learning and research in paediatrics, infant development, and pregnancy, building programmes and initiatives for professionals, parents, and caregivers that shape the future of children's health worldwide.

Through science, we continue to learn more about our youngest and their physical, cognitive, and emotional development. Parents and caregivers want advice on how to use this learning in their daily lives to complement their basic instincts to love, hold, and talk to their babies.

Good parenting is not a one-size-fits-all formula. With JOHNSON'S® *Child Development* series, we hope to support today's families with the knowledge, guidance, and understanding to help them bring forth the miracle embodied in each and every child.

The second year

The beginning of your child's second year is the beginning of a more independent phase, as your baby becomes a toddler. Learning to walk and talk opens up his world, and with you as his guide there is much to explore and discover about his surroundings, his family and friends, and himself. Every day there will be many new experiences to share and enjoy.

Your child's development

You have spent the first year learning to understand and meet your baby's physical and emotional needs, and it's been a very hands-on process. Now the focus changes. This second year is much more about helping your toddler become a self-sufficient individual, branching out into the wider world, with you as a guide.

Your toddler continues to need your active encouragement to explore her capabilities and her surroundings. She will also need you to return to as a safe emotional base because, for all her apparent independence, she needs your love and reassurance.

Developmentally the physical change is enormous. Once your child learns to walk, her horizons expand.

And learning to talk opens up her world to you, and the whole world to her, in a new and exciting way. Your toddler will constantly attempt to move ahead of her immediate capabilities, which may lead to enormous frustration for her. Learning about limits, her own and those set by you, is new for both of you. With patient teaching and encouragement, she can learn to follow basic safety rules and cooperate with your expectations.

Establishing a safe environment

As a baby, your toddler explored things with her hands and this continues, except now the exploration isn't limited to those toys given to her. She can move around her home, and everything is worth investigating, whether it's the dog's bowl, the kitchen cupboards, or the CD player. How can she tell the difference between those buttons she can press and those she can't? It's not possible without your help, so remove items that can be damaged and direct her attention to activities that take advantage of her natural curiosity and pleasure of exploration.

Setting the pace for your toddler

Toddlers cannot self-limit their activity. They tend to move straight from one activity to another without pause and to put every ounce of their energy into each. Your toddler will rely on you to help set the pace, so

that she can manage to enjoy activities without overdoing them to the point of exhaustion, which is sometimes where the flash point of frustration ignites into a tantrum.

Toddlers still need lots of rest, and most will probably continue to need at least one daytime nap for this year. Well-slept and rested toddlers will manage life better than those who are tired. And if your toddler is a poor sleeper at night, don't be tempted to keep her going all day in the hope that she will sleep continuously through the night. The more tired she is, the less easy she will find it to relax into a good sleep pattern.

Ultimately, this is a wonderfully exciting time for you and your toddler, full of new experiences. Understanding what makes your toddler tick, and what her needs are, will help you create those opportunities that bring out the best in her.

About this book

During this thrilling year of change, your support, encouragement, and love can do more than anything else to help your toddler blossom. Understanding how your toddler develops is vital to helping you tune into her needs and give her what she wants.

Section 1
The first half of this book tells you about how your toddler's development will affect both her physical and her emotional needs. For example, why does your 20-month-old keep having tantrums in public places when previously she was well behaved? How important is it that she talks in simple sentences at a certain age? Now she has begun walking, how can you keep her safe?

Being one step ahead in terms of knowing what to expect from your toddler will help you understand her so you can respond in the most effective way possible. And being able to meet her needs in this way will not only help her feel loved and valued but boost your confidence as a parent, too.

At this age safety is so important. This book helps you to prepare a safe environment for your child's continuing development. It discusses how to balance safety issues with allowing your toddler the freedom to explore.

Section 2
The second half of this book contains what you need to know about how and when your toddler is likely to reach each new milestone. Although the information is organized month by month, it's important to remember that the time-scale is flexible. All toddlers develop at different rates, and your toddler will progress at the speed that's right for her.

Once you see your toddler trying to do something new, there are lots of things you can do to try to encourage her along the way, and this section includes ideas for games and activities you can play with her. Giving your toddler the right kind of stimulation at just the right time will build her confidence and self-esteem and help give her the best possible start in life.

Family life

The commitment and unconditional love provided by a family will ensure that a toddler has the best possible start in life. Now, a year after he was born, your toddler may still be the newest member of the family, but he is also very much a personality in his own right, beginning to forge his own independent relationships with other family members.

Sibling relationships

During this second year of your toddler's life you may be having another baby, and this will be a major but positive change in your toddler's life. Your toddler may feel hardly more than a baby himself to you, and you may wonder how he will cope with a new addition. He will take his lead from you, but keep it simple. Don't overplay the benefits of having a brother or sister because it will be some time before they will be able to play together. What he is likely to be most aware of after the new baby arrives is that he won't always be the only one who needs attention. Given that developmentally he is naturally very self-focused, this will take some adjustment on his part. His routine will also be changed. Give him time to adjust, and make sure he still gets some one-to-one time; otherwise his sense of fairness will be

offended too! "Role conflict" may also be a problem for a while, as your toddler gets used to no longer being the "baby" of the family.

If you already have older children, or stepchildren, then the relationship between them and their younger sibling will become even stronger, even if there are squabbles along the way. Many children seem to fight endlessly, but they are, in fact, forming deep emotional attachments and will probably be great friends and allies as adults. In some ways, children get into a habit of communicating by squabbling, so you will need to set some ground rules so they play together harmoniously.

Often an older child will be too "helpful" to his younger sibling. It is frustrating for a toddler who is trying to do something by himself to have someone more competent keep taking his game over. In such a case you may need to point out gently to the older child that the younger child needs more time. However, try not to be too interventionist – your children sometimes need to sort things out between them in their own way.

Position in the family

Numerous studies have been undertaken to understand if birth order has an impact on personality. If your toddler is your first child, you will probably have had more time to spend with him than is ever going to be likely with any subsequent children. However, with first children there is so much for parents to learn about their care and development, which becomes second nature with later children. First-born children tend to be more achievement-orientated, and are often more strong-willed than later children. They have had the unique experience of never having to share their parents' attention, at least for a while, and often have a strong sense of responsibility.

Second and subsequent children often have better social skills because they have always had to share time and attention with another child, and have sometimes had to take a back seat. They also have to learn to manage living with an older child who will always be more competent than they are. While this may be very frustrating, it may allow them to develop other ways to survive unequal competition.

Only children are often very successful in later life because they have had their parents' undivided attention, and been able to focus on their achievements without having to share with siblings.

Twins or more

It is important in the case of multiples to try to spend time individually with each baby. This may be a challenge at first, when the physical care of more than one baby takes up so much time. Enlist the help of another family member, or a childminder, to allow you the time and opportunity to do this.

There are two types of twins: identical and non-identical. The incidence of non-identical multiples has increased in frequency with the use of new fertility treatments. Those children born as a twin or triplet will always have to share. Non-identical or fraternal twins are no more alike than non-twin siblings, but identical twins – who have identical genetic material – will be very similar, although their developing personalities will differ.

Emotional development

Family life is an important arena for emotional development. You will already be familiar with the development of your baby's emotions over the first year. From a very early age your baby learned to express pleasure by smiling. Faced with a surprise or completely unknown situation, she may have shown fear by crying. Secure in your arms, she will have settled calmly and happily, expressing contentment.

Some children are emotionally very responsive, and others less so. Something that one child finds frightening, is merely of interest to another. During the first year of your child's life, you will have learned a lot about how she approaches the world and you will have been able to help create a balance for her between what she can cope with on her own and with what she needs help. Some babies are easily overstimulated and become fretful, needing more calm and soothing tactics than others. Others are more reticent and will need more encouragement to interact or respond to stimuli.

Expressing emotions in security

Your child's love for you is easily expressed. She may return your cuddles and kisses with great pleasure, but will also use you to demonstrate stronger emotions like anger. Often for children the development of a full range of emotions can be almost overwhelming, and can only be expressed within a secure environment. You are that secure environment, and in order to experience strong emotions she will need you to help her manage them because she isn't yet able to do so for herself.

You will learn what is best for your child, and it is your role to learn from her cues. Sometimes when children are angry, it may be beneficial to hold them in order to help them contain their feelings, talking calmly all the while. Some children respond better to being left alone until they feel better. But, after any emotional outburst, all toddlers need to be reassured with a loving cuddle.

The role of imaginative play

Apart from the immediate expression of emotions such as happiness, fear, and anger, which are relatively straightforward and easy to recognize in your child, she will begin to imitate expressions of love and concern for others. Being encouraged to demonstrate expressions of affection or sympathy for others, even if she doesn't actually feel it yet, helps with the development of these feelings of empathy. She may also act out different emotions with her teddies or dolls, practising them through her play. This is very important because it means she can experience difficult feelings in a safe place through her imaginative play and begin to understand what it is like to consider other people's feelings.

Relating to others

What you will notice during the course of this year is that your toddler's pleasure and appreciation of events will begin to include other people. Her excitement at going to a parent and toddler group, for example, will start to reflect her enjoyment and enthusiasm for spending time with particular friends. She may enjoy going to Granny's or visiting another family member because she is developing a close and loving relationship, independent of you, with that person.

All these experiences are helping her to develop a full and satisfying emotional life, where she can express her feelings in the safe context of knowing that she is loved and that they are validated. You can make her feel secure no matter what emotions she is expressing.

ACTING OUT EMOTIONS
This toddler is pretending her much-loved soft toy monkey, Timmy, is tired and needs to have a nap. She puts him to sleep on his back, and makes soothing noises to quieten him ready for sleep.

Managing separation

Allowing your child to develop other relationships – with relatives or childminders – independently of you is very beneficial and will help her manage separation from you. Many toddlers are still showing separation anxiety at this age, and every child will experience it at some point. So take it slowly. Start by playing simple games, such as peekaboo, to help her to understand that things that go away will come back.

You can help your toddler believe that she can manage without you for a while by providing her with the experience of doing so. Encourage her to spend time with other loved adults away from home as well as at home. Suggest that she take along a favourite toy or security object for extra reassurance. Even if she finds it hard at first, it will help her self-confidence in the long run. Above all, try not to convey to her that she is totally dependent on you or to impose on her your own anxiety about being separated from her.

Social development

During this second year, your toddler is inclined to see life with himself right at its centre. This egocentricity is essential to establishing the secure self-image that will eventually enable him to extend his consideration to other children and adults. Help him build on his self-image and become more sensitive to other people's needs by ensuring that you meet his needs.

A lot of social development happens at home quite naturally within the context of family and friends. And when there are siblings, there will probably be less need for your intervention. It's sometimes helpful to allow siblings to sort out their differences between themselves.

This day-to-day social interaction with other children at home is not available to first-born or only children, and needs to be sought elsewhere. Initially, this will be through children of parental friends, visits to the park, and parent and toddler groups. In a group of children

where most are older, some of the problems that arise between toddlers won't come up, and this can be an easier environment in some ways to begin social acclimatization. However, he will begin to work out ways of interacting socially with his peer group when he reaches a pre-school environment next year.

Teaching your toddler to share

Alongside your toddler's self-focus comes a strong streak of possessiveness, all of which makes social interaction a bit of a minefield amongst similar-aged children!

The concept of sharing is difficult for toddlers to grasp, so don't expect them to be able to do it willingly at first. Remember that the ability to share comes from feeling secure inside. So, instead of focusing too closely on the issue of sharing, try the following: remove toys "for later" that are being squabbled over; ignore bad reactions as far as possible; and look out for opportunities to reward and reinforce occasions when one child willingly relinquishes a toy to another. It may not happen out of any inclination to share at first, but it gives you a chance to praise this sort of behaviour, and toddlers respond better to praise than to anger and irritation on your part.

IT'S MY TOY!
This little boy doesn't want anyone else to have his toy, even though he doesn't want to use it himself at the moment. He fears that he will never get the toy back if he lets someone else have it. Learning to share requires careful management by his carers.

Considering child care

Being looked after by someone other than a parent, or close family member, can be positively beneficial for your child once you have found the right person or facility. However, it is important to consider what your child's needs are, and how best these can be met, bearing in mind that toddlers need lots of one-to-one attention, particularly to encourage language development.

There are several child care options to choose from. A nanny who comes to your home or a childminder who lives close by may be one option to explore. Interview any possible candidates thoroughly and check their references. Family members who live nearby may also be an option. You will need to find someone who is warm and attentive to your child, and has ideas and values similar to your own. Do not expect someone to care for your child exactly as you would: the relationship will inevitably be different.

A workplace creche or nursery may suit your requirements. Ask your local authority for a list of registered child care services. Visit several to gain an understanding of each one's approach to child care, and ensure that the manager and staff are properly qualified.

Discipline

Discipline is not the same as punishment. Discipline is about teaching your toddler what is expected of her, both within the family and in wider society. It is about setting consistent limits and understanding that your toddler's constant testing of these is part of how she will learn to accept them. It should always be done with love and respect for your toddler.

Don't expect too much obedience of your toddler. Remember that she still has lots to learn about good behaviour and consideration of others. Her learning will be gradual as she has a very short memory span and does not recall "lessons" except through repeated experience. At the moment she is very self-centred, and a lot of her behaviour, which you may consider naughty, is just an extension of exploring some of the new things she can do, and seeing how far your limits extend.

What also has to be respected is that a young child cannot always make herself understood, especially when it comes to explaining how she is feeling. Sometimes a child will test the limits when feeling anxious, in which case your toddler will need attention and reassurance, not punishment. Thinking about the world from a toddler's point of view, and being sensitive to situations that might be stressful for your child, helps you to see their behaviour in perspective.

A positive approach

Discipline requires a positive approach, using lots of praise and encouragement, and setting a good example through adult behaviour. You cannot expect a child to learn that hitting is not okay if you smack her. That is not

consistent behaviour and will only give mixed messages. If you want your toddler to behave well, it is important to notice when she does, and to praise her for it. Don't wait until she annoys you and then get cross, or she will learn that the only way to get your attention is to behave badly rather than well. Noticing good behaviour and commenting specifically about it is important. Your toddler wants to please you for the same reason she

Avoiding confrontation

You can help prevent some unnecessary daily confrontations by doing a few simple things. For example, you could move precious objects, and the plant that she enjoys pulling the leaves off, out of her reach. And you could get a security cover to prevent her posting her toys inside the video player that is so similar to her postbox toy. Your aim should be to provide your toddler (and her friends) with a safe environment in which to play, where she can do little damage to valued possessions.

cannot be expected of your child yet. Self-discipline comes from learning to manage and control your feelings and impulses, and is linked to self-motivation and self-esteem. If, through positive discipline, you can help your toddler learn that it is a particular sort of behaviour that gets attention and praise, what we would describe as good behaviour, you are sowing the seeds for her ability to manage her behaviour well in the future.

Remember that your toddler's behaviour is simply the way she learns. Allow her plenty of time, and offer her understanding and guidance.

smiled back at you when she was a baby: she loves you, and pleasing you makes her feel good. Praising her efforts shows your respect and validation of her efforts, which will also help develop her self-esteem.

Effective intervention

Distraction is often a successful technique to use when your toddler will not cooperate. For example, if your toddler refuses to put on a coat, distract her with a toy, and then put the coat on her while she's looking at it.

Giving your toddler a choice is also very effective. For example, when she refuses to put on the coat, try asking her, "Do you want to put this arm in first or this arm?"

You should ignore some of your toddler's unwanted behaviour to avoid it becoming attention-seeking. If your toddler deliberately throws a toy car, which may hit another child, explain that such behaviour is unacceptable and that you must intervene.

Combining the techniques

All of these strategies take time and patience, but be reassured that by using them you are helping your toddler learn some very positive lessons for life. Learning about discipline is also the beginning of learning about self-discipline, although this takes years to develop and

Tantrums

Tantrums are an expression of the overwhelming frustration felt by a young child, who doesn't yet have the emotional maturity to deal with such strong feelings. With all his new physical skills, it is right that he should want to explore his capabilities, but when he discovers there is something he can't manage, or isn't allowed, then the frustration can become too much to cope with.

Most tantrums occur around the age of 20 months. They often happen when there is a clash of interests – his desire for more independence, and your desire to keep him safe, for example. At this age, children can understand but not express themselves well. Tantrums can be very difficult to deal with, especially as the physical expression of anger can be difficult to watch.

To be overwhelmed by his feelings is also a surprising experience for your toddler, and he will need you to help him feel comforted and secure after it is over, even if you pay him minimal attention while it's happening (especially the first time it occurs).

Your toddler is more likely to have a tantrum away from home; for example, when you're in a shop or at

• Does he find it impossible to deal with the supermarket shop at the end of a day? Then try taking him in the morning instead and keeping the visit brief, or leaving him with a minder while you go shopping.

It isn't fair to ask him to manage situations that are beyond his emotional capabilities without some consideration of his needs, and it's easier for you, too, in the long run. Remember that tantrums are linked to this developmental phase and will pass.

Being reasonable

Try not to get yourself locked into a situation of saying "No" every time a request comes up. Be firm and consistent but also be reasonable.

The trick is to set the sort of limits that allow your child to develop greater independence from you, without also letting tantrums become an attention-seeking habit. Like many parenting skills, this takes thought and practice as you learn to "read" this next stage of your toddler's development, which is the beginning of a change from dependence to independence.

a friend's house. This is because he's feeling insecure. He may be feeling less secure when away from home because your attention is less closely focused on him, and this makes his frustrations overwhelming. It's difficult enough to make yourself understood when you aren't yet proficient at talking, but doubly so if your parent is distracted. At least when he is at home he feels secure, and probably has better access to your attention, so a tantrum may be less likely to happen there.

Minimizing the incidence of tantrums

It is also worth thinking about those situations that you know your child finds difficult at the moment. These can lead to the sorts of frustrations that can result in a tantrum.
• For example, does he find it difficult to deal with groups of people when he is tired? If so, either schedule events that involve others after a nap, or make sure he isn't overwhelmed in such a situation.

Dealing with tantrums

If a full-blown tantrum occurs, it may help to just sit it out, as long as your child is not in danger. Some children will need to be held tight and talked to in a reassuring voice. Losing control yourself doesn't help at all, and may just prolong the unwanted behaviour. Shouting at and smacking your child isn't appropriate, and is about as effective in dealing with the problem as having a tantrum yourself.

Thinking about how it feels from his point of view sometimes helps take the heat out of the situation. Diversionary tactics can sometimes head off a tantrum, either by walking away and ignoring a situation that you know could escalate, or distracting him with an alternative suggestion, keeping the mood calm and light.

Developmental check

Between 18 and 24 months you should take your child for a developmental and health check, which provides you with a good opportunity to ensure that all is going well, and to raise any concerns you might have. This check-up may be carried out by your health visitor, but it is more likely to be done by a community paediatrician, who has specialist training in child development.

Assessing physical development

Your child will be weighed and measured, and this will be checked against a standard chart and your child's previous measurements, to ensure that growth is appropriate for her. You may be asked about what

sorts of foods she enjoys eating now, and the doctor may make suggestions that are helpful to you. Her teeth will probably be checked to see how they are coming through, and you may be asked about taking your child to visit the dentist.

Her eyes and ears will be checked, and possibly her heart. Hearing is important for learning to talk, and if your child is too shy to talk to the doctor you will probably be asked about her speech. At this age, her social interaction and understanding is more important than what she is actually saying.

Assessing your child's skills

You will probably be asked various routine questions about what your child is capable of doing now. The doctor will assess her physical skills by watching her walk, and asking her to do simple play tasks like balancing a block one on top of another. These activities demonstrate her gross and fine motor skills (control of large-scale and more precise movements). The doctor may also show her pictures of different objects and ask her, "Which one is the cat?", for example, to test her comprehension. She may also be asked other simple questions about other pictures or items.

WORD RECOGNITION
The health visitor holds up a picture of a cat and another of a dog and asks the toddler to point to the picture of the cat. She identifies the cat without hesitation: her comprehension is good.

DEVELOPING FINE MOTOR SKILLS
The toddler is then given three bricks and asked to build them into a tower. She concentrates as she picks up each brick in turn and carefully and precisely positions one on top of the other.

A chance for discussion

This routine check-up will also be an opportunity to talk through any worries you may have about your child's development, eating habits, sleeping patterns, potty training, behaviour, and general health.

As toddlers are in more social settings with other children, they tend to get more colds or minor health problems as their immune system starts to get to grips with common infections. If your toddler seems to continually suffer from coughs and colds, you may want advice about how you can help boost her general health. In addition, such illnesses, if left untreated, could lead to hearing problems. If you have concerns about hearing or language development, talk to your doctor about them.

Behavioural development

If your child is consistently under the weather, or gets very tired, it can affect her behaviour. A toddler who hasn't had enough sleep over a consistent period will find it difficult to focus on behaving well, and will become frustrated and overwhelmed. Consider what your toddler needs physically, in order to develop emotionally. If you have reduced her daytime naps, for example, bring bedtime forward. Tired toddlers also have less interest in eating, so try to organize mealtimes for when your child is more alert, to avoid possible behavioural problems.

Immunization

There are a number of immunizations that are recommended during the second year, including the measles, mumps, and rubella vaccination (MMR). In the US, this is mandatory for school entry. Also in the US, the Varicella vaccination that immunizes against chickenpox is recommended.

In addition, there are recommendations for booster doses of those immunizations given during the first year. These include DTP (diphtheria, tetanus, and pertussis), polio, Hib (against the virus that can cause meningitis), and in the US this recommendation also includes a booster vaccination against hepatitis B. If you have any reservations about immunization, then take this opportunity to talk them through with your doctor.

Potty training

You cannot train a child to use his potty until his nervous system is developed enough to control the bowel and bladder sphincter muscles. This generally happens between 18 and 36 months, with girls tending to be ready before boys.

In the past babies were regularly sat on potties, until they had passed water, which avoided at least one wet nappy while giving the impression that they were being "trained". Predicting a time when you know your child is likely to have a bowel movement, for example after eating, and sitting him on his potty then until he does so may teach him that this is what his potty is for, but it won't teach him to control his bowel movements. That will only happen when he is developmentally ready.

In addition, it won't be possible to potty train your child until he is aware of the sensation of wanting to go, is physically able to control the urge until he reaches the potty, and can sit down safely on it. All these skills have to be mastered before you can expect your child to manage without nappies.

Beginning training

Look out for signs of training readiness, which suggest that it might be worth introducing the idea. These include being aware of having a wet nappy or of doing a bowel movement, or sometimes having a dry nappy for a long period, which indicates that your child's bladder is able to store urine in larger quantities. Your child may also show an inclination to copy you by volunteering to use a potty.

In summer months, allow your child to play outside without his nappy on. Without a nappy on, doing a wee is much more obvious! And this will help him to

Introducing the potty

Your first step, at around 18 months, will be to introduce your child to the idea of what will be expected of him in future months.

★ You can do this by having a potty around, close to the family toilet so the association is made, and letting him sit on it perhaps before his bath in the evening, after you have taken off his nappy. Don't expect him to use it, but just to get used to the idea of sitting on it. If something happens while he's sitting on it, great.

★ In a family that is quite relaxed about using the toilet, in which your child has seen you using it, it's easier for him to make the connection. Place the potty next to the toilet and encourage him to sit on it when you go to the toilet.

★ Choose a potty that won't tip up when being sat on, or when your child stands up. For boys, it is helpful to get one designed with a higher splashguard at the front; this will help ensure that his penis is pointing down into the bowl of the potty. Boys will probably want to stand up to wee in the toilet in time, but because a bowel movement is usually accompanied by passing water, starting off with a potty is probably easier for him at first.

★ Avoid a heavy emphasis on success and failure, as it will be counterproductive. Remind yourself that this is about introducing the idea of using the potty, not producing a toilet-trained child. Give praise when deserved, and be patient.

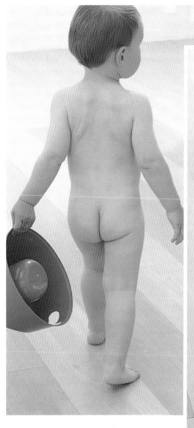

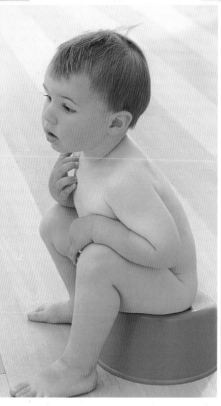

understand what it is you are referring to when you ask him if he wants to do a wee. For boys, imitation is important, so let him watch his father or older brother use the toilet.

Make sure you don't give mixed messages about your child's bowel movements. It's confusing to him if you praise his efforts, then say they are nasty or dirty. Be positive about any successes, but deliberately ignore accidents when they occur. Your child really cannot help himself and, because children focus so exclusively on one thing at a time, even when he is trained there are still bound to be accidents sometimes.

Above all, don't get emotionally fraught about the process, which can become all too common if you start trying to potty-train your child before he is ready. If your child is having repeated accidents then stop, and go back to nappies for a few weeks. Don't attempt to move from nappies to pants at any time of stress. It's not fair to ask your child to deal with too much at once – wait for a more settled time.

Controlling the bowels

You may find that even when your child is happy to use the potty for passing water, having a bowel movement is a different proposition, and he may want to continue doing this in a nappy. From his point of view, it is quite a different sensation doing this on the potty or toilet to doing it in a nappy, and some children find it a bit strange. Often, they will wait until they have had their night-time nappy put on before evacuating their bowels. Although this can be rather frustrating, try to stay calm. Your child's anxiety will pass in time. Do not hurry him.

Toddlers in action

The toddler years are often years of great physical activity. Now that she is mobile, and curious, your toddler will want to find out about what she is capable of and the world about her. She may seem to have a "Go" button but no "Stop" button. Help your toddler learn to manage her energy as constructively as possible, because this is an important step in her development.

Toddlers have lots of energy and masses of curiosity. They love practising their newly mastered walking and running skills, and enjoy exploring their environment fully. So, it is important to allow your toddler plenty of time to run around in a safe space, such as a park, playground, or indoor soft-play area. Take a ball with you to kick and chase.

The importance of physical activity

Channel your child's energy constructively as well as allowing for free play in the park or with other children. At this age, learning how to swim provides a good opportunity to become physically competent in water. Music and movement is also popular: it develops concentration, coordination, rhythm, and imagination if you devise different games for the music. There are also toddler gym classes and indoor soft-play facilities that allow toddlers to improve their balance and motor skills as they develop muscle strength and have fun.

The difference between boys and girls

Numerous studies have shown that boys need more physical activity than girls. Boys tend to become more restless more often and concentrate for shorter periods on quieter activities (such as playing with blocks or toy animals) than girls. If your toddler is a boy, when he becomes restless or frustrated instigate a short period of physical activity, such as a walk round the block with his

Calming activities

★ Sitting together and reading a book to your child is one excellent way of using a peaceful activity to promote closeness, while providing an opportunity for your child to practise her listening and concentration skills.

★ Drawing and scribbling with crayons, or painting with a brush, is another absorbing activity that requires you to stay peacefully in one place.

★ Listening to soft, gentle music while being cuddled is another way of helping your toddler to relax.

★ A warm bath, a familiar activity since birth, can be physically relaxing, which helps calm things down.

★ Gentle massage helps a lot of children. It helps them regain a sense of their physical selves. You can gently massage the feet, with or without baby oil, moving up the legs. A gentle head massage while she rests in your lap can feel wonderful as it releases tension in the neck and scalp muscles, while circular clockwise stroking of the abdomen can reduce stress in the stomach.

push-along trolley or a game of being chased by you in the garden or park. Once he has let off steam, he will be happy to sit down with his crayons or toy cars again.

Recharging the batteries

Try to balance periods where your toddler expends physical energy with quieter times that allow her to relax and recharge her batteries. A toddler who knows how to relax will also find settling down to sleep easier than one who does not. Children who consistently do not get enough sleep are often overactive because they become physically reliant on excess "awake" hormones to compensate for lack of sleep.

Small children have immature nervous systems and are easily overstimulated. An overstimulated toddler becomes frustrated when playing, requiring more intervention than usual. When this happens, involve your toddler in a quiet, soothing activity, such as reading a book. If she is consistently tired by lunchtime or early afternoon, try putting her in her cot for a daytime nap, to improve her energy levels for the rest of the day.

You may find that your child's energy levels are revitalized after eating. Small children easily flag without regular refuelling. Concentrate on giving her healthy snacks, and limit highly processed foods and those that contain a lot of chemical additives.

Sleeping

During the second year, toddlers need about 12 to 14 hours sleep within a 24-hour period. Sleep is very important to babies, and deep sleep is necessary for all children, as it is restorative and helps to promote growth.

Getting enough sleep

Ideally toddlers need a long period of uninterrupted sleep at night and one or two naps during the day. However, it is worth bearing in mind that, without adequate sleep, your toddler may find it hard to do all the growing and developing that this busy second year demands. A well-slept toddler is more able to make use of the time spent awake than a toddler who is cranky.

We are all too well aware of how we feel when we don't get enough sleep, and it's the same for your child. If you are concerned that your toddler is not getting enough sleep, especially on a regular basis, look for the signs in his behaviour. Is his hand–eye coordination less efficient that usual, making him misjudge movements slightly? Does he have tantrums more frequently? Is he more withdrawn and less sociable? Do games always seem to end in tears? Does he have little enthusiasm for going to the park, where formerly he was always keen? If the answer to several of these questions is "Yes", then he probably isn't getting enough sleep, and you should speak to your healthcare professional. Remember that toddlers can recharge their batteries during quiet periods – they do not always have to be asleep to do this.

Establishing a sleeping pattern

It is through the regular occurrence of different daily activities – getting up, mealtimes, nap times, and bedtime – that your child learns about the difference between day and night. As children's brains mature, their internal circadian rhythms adapt to the patterns of life they experience. So, if you want them to adapt to a pattern that suits you – sleeping through the night, for example – they have to experience how.

Your toddler's bedtime and waking patterns will have some influence on what times suit you and him for naps. You may find your toddler can keep going during the morning, have an early lunch, and then a good two-hour sleep in the early afternoon, before bed at seven in the evening. Alternatively, if your child wakes very early, a long morning nap and a short one in the middle of the afternoon works best. Although your routine will probably change over this year, as your child's sleep at night improves and the daytime sleep needs drop, a routine is helpful to your child. However, there may be days when you need to be more flexible.

Introducing a bedtime routine

One of the ways in which you can help your child learn about sleeping well through the night is by having a bedtime routine. If this isn't already a feature of your family life, it will be as well to introduce it now, because you want your child to get a good night's sleep and to learn that going to bed is in itself a good and pleasurable activity at the end of a busy day.

★ Don't wait until your child is overtired before you start the bedtime routine: it should be a calm and relaxed period of the day, leading gently towards the inevitability of bed and sleep.

★ If you have bathed your baby in the morning during the first year, try moving this wonderfully relaxing activity to the end of the day. A bath before bedtime will not only help your child to wind down, it will also – if it becomes a part of his daily routine – mean that your child will begin to associate having a bath with bedtime. It will thus become a gentle preparation for sleep.

★ Your routine might follow a pattern like this: About an hour after your toddler has his last meal of the day, you give him a bath, allowing him time to play. After the bath, you sit down quietly together and you read him a bedtime story, before gently putting him to bed.

★ It is consistency in the daily bedtime routine that is important, so if some elements of the routine need to be done by a caregiver, make sure she knows what they are. Routine helps create the security that allows your toddler to get into his bed happily, and fall asleep by himself.

If your child wakes very early, or is wakeful at night, don't be tempted to drop the day-time naps in order to try to increase night-time tiredness. Overtired children find sleep more of a problem than those who are generally well slept. When children don't get enough sleep for long periods of time, they come to rely on stress hormones to keep them going. This can make them cranky and overactive. If your child finds sleep difficult, he needs help to learn to sleep better, not less sleep.

If the bedtime routine seems a little difficult to you, it may be because you are starting it too late. Start it a little earlier when, being less tired, it may make it possible to manage the idea of bedtime more easily. And, if he has missed or had a shorter daytime nap for any reason,

aim to put him to bed a little earlier to compensate. The idea is that your child will be so calm and contented that he will be able to go to sleep in his own bed and by himself. All of which may take consistency and patience.

Dealing with night waking

When children of around a year old wake at night, many of them will not simply turn over and go back to sleep but will wake their parents up as well! Children generally will compensate for losing sleep at night by sleeping for longer during daytime naps. However, this will probably not be an option for you and you may well prefer to enjoy the day with your baby and for all the family to sleep well at night.

Habitual waking

If your child has got into the habit of night waking – because this is what it is, a habit – you can help him change it. There is seldom any other reason for night waking, other than during periods of ill-health, that isn't caused by not having learned to be self-sufficient, so that he is unable to get himself back off to sleep without your assistance. For example, if you have got into the habit of feeding your baby until he falls asleep, or holding or rocking him, he will be unable to fall asleep by himself if he wakes in the night. Given that a baby is on a 50-minute sleep cycle, compared to an adult's 90-minute one, this can mean regular wakings during the night, when you are needed to help your child get back to sleep.

What you need to do is give your child the opportunity of learning how to be self-sufficient, and allow him to learn how to go to sleep by himself. If he has learned how to sleep with you cuddling him, he can learn a new routine with your patience and commitment. This means that when, during his 50-minute sleep cycle, he hits a patch of light sleep and half-wakes or wakes, he

will go back to sleep by himself. This is what we all do, every night. He may be disinclined to learn this new skill, because he is familiar with what he knows, but everyone in the family benefits if you help him make this change.

Making a new habit

As well as making sure that the bedtime routine is now a feature, which should help him adjust to this new idea of sleeping throughout the night, you will also have to reduce all stimulation at night when he does wake. This includes breast-feeding him or giving him any sort of bottle at night. He may ask for a bottle or a feed because he associates this with going to sleep, but, unlike the first year, you don't need to give him a bottle during the night as he gets all the calories he needs during the day. Feeding now will only stimulate his digestive system and disrupt his sleep pattern further.

In order for your toddler to learn how to get to sleep by himself, you may have to tolerate his protests and tears for a short period. Many parents find it helpful to

SECURITY TOYS OR BLANKETS
This little girl always takes her two much-loved dolls to bed with her. Their familiarity is comforting and gives her enough security to let you go. Many toddlers use a piece of blanket as their comforter.

Bad dreams

Bad dreams are thought to be unusual before the age of two, but if your toddler wakes during the night and is very distressed, it is possible that he may have been frightened by a bad dream. His developing imagination, combined with an inability to distinguish between imagined and real events, may cause him to panic as he remembers his bad dream on waking. Go and comfort him, and reassure him that he is in no real danger.

Dreaming occurs during REM (rapid eye movement) sleep, which occurs after the first four hours of sleep. If your toddler cries out in fright before then, he may be experiencing a night terror. Night terrors are very rare, and occur during deep, non-dreaming sleep. Your toddler may appear to be awake but actually he is still asleep and will have no memory of the event later.

bring about change gradually. What is important is that you are consistent. So, next time he wakes and asks for milk, say "No" gently but firmly, tuck him in again, and leave the room. If he cries, as is likely, wait for five minutes before going back into his room. Reassure him, but again say "No" to his request, and do not get him up. Tuck him in again, and leave the room. Increase the time you stay away by five minutes after each visit, up to 20 minutes, until he has fallen asleep.

Leaving your child to cry for 10 minutes or so will do him no lasting harm if it is within the context of your loving care. He won't be able to learn what is expected of him unless you are consistent, so don't give in halfway through. It sometimes helps to start by leaving him to go to sleep on his own during his daytime nap, as you will be less tired during the day.

Feeding

By the end of the first year, your child should be eating mainly family meals, although prepared with less salt or sugar than for an adult. She will bite and chew with her gums a long time before teeth appear, using the copious saliva she also produces to help soften foods. In fact, chewing and biting with the gums helps to promote the proper alignment of teeth as they come through.

By now you will be offering your toddler food that needs to be chewed, even if it is often chopped up in small, bite-sized pieces. In addition, offer soft foods from which she can take a bite; for example, pieces of banana.
● Introduce new foods one by one to make certain your toddler is not allergic to them.

● Certain food items are best avoided, as they run the risk of choking – peanuts, whole grapes, boiled sweets, large pieces of raw carrot, for example.
● Never leave a toddler who is eating unattended, and never allow her to eat while on the move.

Feeding herself

You can probably expect your toddler to feed herself with finger foods pretty well by now, and this will improve dramatically over the year as her hand–eye skills and her coordination and dexterity improve. She may be quite slow, especially to start with, and is unlikely to sit down and just eat – sometimes preferring to play with her food! – but, even if haphazard, using a spoon competently is possible at this age. You may need to help her finish off what's in her bowl, or feed her the occasional spoonful as she feeds herself, but by and large she should be able to manage by herself.

Providing foods that can be eaten by hand – pieces of fruit, or little sandwiches, for example – also helps her feel that she is becoming more independent and that should please her and make her want to eat, too.

Balancing liquids and solids

In addition to being able to feed herself, your child should be drinking regularly from a cup – even if you start with a feeder beaker. Bottles should now be a thing of the past, and if you are still breast-feeding this may be limited now to morning and evening feeds.

If your child is still having large quantities of milk during the day, which helps her feel "full up" very quickly, she may not develop enough of an appetite for her meals. At this age two to three glasses of whole milk per day is more than enough. She may prefer drinking milk to eating solids, which is more time-consuming and less immediately satisfying in terms of feeling full. Encourage her to concentrate on solids at mealtimes and offer her some milk after she has eaten.

Drinking large quantities of juice can have a similar effect, especially as the sugar content in fruit juice is high. It may also cause diarrhoea and will increase the risk of tooth cavities. Drinking a lot of fruit juice now will give your toddler the expectation of high-sugar foods later

on. Limit her intake to 100g (4oz) a day. One very effective way of doing this is to dilute her drinks of fruit juice with water.

Eating together

When it comes to helping your toddler see what is expected of her at mealtimes, it helps if you sit and eat together, perhaps not at every meal but certainly once a day. At this age it is through imitation, and imitating the behaviour of those close to her, that your child is learning about her world and what happens in it.

Sitting together over a meal is a great time for family interaction and starting a routine. It also provides your toddler with the opportunity to learn how to behave appropriately at the table by imitating other members of the family. If you don't do this at home, it will be difficult for her to know how to do it if you go out to a relative's or a restaurant. And, while you cannot expect a toddler to tolerate a three-course, sit-down meal, you can help her join in and eat, and spend some of that time at the table contributing to the social occasion of the meal and family interaction.

Meeting your child's needs

What might seem a bit mysterious to you is that, in spite of all the physical activity that is so characteristic of the toddler years, your child appears to want to eat less. This is because her growth rate has slowed down in comparison to the first year. Over three meals, two drinks of milk and the occasional healthy snack during the day, her needs are easily met. Follow her lead and let her eat according to her appetite, while always offering her healthy choices.

You may also find that your child's eating habits are a bit erratic; she may eat very well some days and hardly at all on others. Don't worry about such discrepancies. Take a longer-term view, and assess what she has eaten over the course of a week. You will probably find that overall she has eaten about the right amount.

Making choices

Your toddler's sense of taste will be more developed now, and she may well start expressing a preference for one food over another. Try to encourage her to eat roughly the same foods as you and the rest of the family. This may mean a rethink of your own dietary approach, ensuring that you are giving her the right balance of nutrients. Keep the range of what you offer her to eat wide, and expect some rejections – you can always try a particular food again later.

To help your toddler feel that she has some autonomy over her food, you may wish to offer her a choice of foods at one mealtime. Allow her to choose between two items at first, say an apple or an orange, rather than giving her a handful of items to choose from.

Don't overreact when your toddler rejects your food: it is seldom more than a statement of not wanting it then. Never force-feed your child and try to avoid struggles by keeping mealtimes short – 15 to 30 minutes. If you feel your child has not eaten enough, offer her a healthy snack of cheese or fruit one or two hours later. Three small meals and two healthy snacks a day is fine.

Some children go through quite long phases of refusing certain foods. Don't worry about such phases. If the overall diet is balanced (even if it contains much of the same foods time and time again) and your toddler is happy, healthy, and growing well, then simply go on offering different items without comment.

Looking after your toddler's teeth

As soon as the teeth start to come in, they are susceptible to tooth decay. And by the start of your toddler's second year she will have enough teeth to warrant cleaning at

A healthy diet

Try to use as many fresh ingredients as you can for meals, because processed foods tend to be very high in salt, sugars, and artificial flavourings. Choose foods from the four basic food groups.

★ Meat, fish, eggs, and other protein foods

★ Milk, cheese, yoghurt, and other dairy products

★ Rice, cereals, potatoes, yams, sweet potatoes, bread, pasta, and other carbohydrates

★ Fruits and vegetables

Your child needs protein for growth, carbohydrates and fats for energy, while fruit and vegetables supply vitamins and fibre.

Fat and fibre issues

Remember that the low-fat, high-fibre diet that is suitable for an adult isn't suitable for a child who needs foods that are calorie-dense (weight for weight, they contain more calories) – full-fat milk rather than skimmed, for example.

As long as she is eating a proportion of fresh fruit and vegetables during the day, you don't need to select fibre-rich foods either. These are likely to increase the speed with which food moves through her system, not allowing enough time for all the nutrients to be absorbed. Small children who show signs of malnutrition or iron deficiency in developed countries have often been fed a low-fat, high-fibre diet.

least twice a day – morning and night – and visiting the dentist every six months for a check-up and advice.

You can help avoid cavities in your toddler's teeth by introducing teeth-cleaning. Cavities form when the naturally occurring bacteria in the mouth combine with sugars in the food residues left on the teeth, producing

an acid that attacks the tooth enamel. Avoid extensive snacking on foods, which means that the mouth constantly contains residual sugars. For healthy teeth, it is better to eat at mealtimes, followed by a drink of water or teeth-cleaning, than to snack constantly.

Although these are your toddler's first teeth they are very important, as they help form the mouth and create the space for the second teeth.

Sensible drinking habits

Another culprit in the creation of tooth cavities, or caries, in young children is drinking from bottles, which bathe the mouth in milk (which contains the sugar lactose), or drinking fruit juices (which contain the sugar fructose, even if they are labelled sugar-free).

Drinking from a cup is much better for the teeth at this age, and always offer water as a drink alternative to milk or fruit juices. Tap water is perfectly safe after the first birthday – you don't need to boil and cool it now. Don't give your child mineral water, however, because the mineral content is likely to be too high for her more sensitive system.

Communication skills

Your child will have been communicating with you for a long time before he says his first recognizable word. His language development began when he first heard your voice. He has been communicating with you through his body language and verbally through his babbling and his cries. He has also become adept at interpreting your tones and some of what you say, especially when associated with expressions of affection, or instructions.

What happens when your toddler starts to talk is the coming together of a lot of skills, which combine comprehension and the physical ability to make sound into verbal language. Your child will have been practising making sounds almost since birth, and you will be familiar with his making letter sounds repeatedly, like "b-b-b-b-b", babbling, blowing bubbles, and experimenting with the sounds he can make, and also varying the pitch and volume, perhaps shouting for attention. You can see how much your child understands, even if he cannot talk to you yet, by asking him "Where?" questions, such as, "Where are your feet?" He will probably have no difficulty in showing you!

First words

Although you can expect your child to begin speaking in his second year, there is a large variation between children, even those who are of similar intelligence. It is partly to do with personality and temperament: some children have more verbal personalities than others. In addition, boys tend to talk later than girls, and girls tend to talk more, but on average children produce their first word at around a year old. This may just be a repeated sound that has meaning for them, for example "woof" whenever they see a dog, or a picture of a dog. "Mama" and "Dada" are also common examples. Any words said may well be accompanied by a hand gesture to indicate the object, or to attract your attention to his attempts to speak. First words can cover a wide range of meaning at first, so that "woof" is not only applied to all dogs, but also to all four-legged animals. Also,

The crucial role of hearing in language development

There is one very important requirement to speech and that is the ability to hear. Even if your toddler can hear perfectly, he still needs to be able to distinguish different word sounds free from the interference of any background noise.

It is very important that your toddler engages in a lot of one-to-one communication, without distraction, so that he gets the benefit of hearing clearly not only what is being said but also the sounds of words. Not only will this help him to copy what he hears accurately, but it will also train his brain to distinguish what sounds make up each word. This will help him later when he starts to read, write, and spell. So, make sure that the television or radio isn't providing a constant background noise: turn it off unless you are actually listening to it or watching something. Your child isn't as able as you are to screen out noise when he tries to listen, and needs to hear words clearly.

Without being able to hear, it is impossible for a child to learn to talk, which is dependent on hearing and imitating sounds in a way that enables you to be understood. This is why hearing tests, at birth and again at around eight and 18 months of age, are very important. The earlier a hearing problem is picked up, the better for the child and

MUSICAL WRIST TOY
This toddler is exploring the various sounds that a simple musical wrist toy can make. Listening to words and music is crucial in language development.

his development. Even recurrent ear infections and glue ear can adversely affect your child's ability to hear, and consequently his language development. If your toddler has an ear infection, take him to the doctor's.

if you show a child of this age a picture of a dog sitting down, he may not identify it as a dog because the necessary four legs that help him define a dog are not seen. Your toddler may use one word to describe a range of objects without distinguishing between them, for example, "duck" may be used for all plastic toys and not applied to the real thing at first.

First sentences

First words are followed by two-word statements, which are often requests or commands; for example, "Go away" or "Want it". This will progress to simple sentences such as, "Tom wants teddy", as your toddler's understanding

and vocabulary build. Over your toddler's second year you can expect his verbal skills to develop from first words to telegraphed sentences, in which only the crucial nouns and verbs are spoken. This in turn helps his understanding because, now that he can communicate his interest in something more explicitly, he gets more detailed verbal information from you.

Television isn't recommended for this age group. Its fast-moving images are very attractive, but the speech is generally too difficult to follow, making it a language-free form of entertainment. So, if your toddler is spending a large amount of time watching television, it will probably have a negative effect on his language development.

Encouraging language development

The connection between language development and a later ability to read and write has been proved quite conclusively in research studies. Two or three one-to-one sessions daily between adult and child, of 10 or 15 minutes each, in which a baby or young child is talked to, read to, or sung to, without any background noise, has an enormously positive impact. Children who have received this sort of input show a reading age of almost 18 months ahead of their peer group at the age of seven.

The reason it makes such a difference is because the ability to hear different letter sounds, after your child has learned the individual letters of the alphabet and their sounds, makes it easier to identify them when they are seen written down. The words "fat" and "mat" have a very distinctive ending sound of "at" but, because of the different letter at the beginning, two very different meanings. Being able to distinguish between letter sounds becomes more important later when learning to spell.

It is fine for your child to hear two languages being spoken at home as long as specific individuals always speak the same language; for example, his grandmother always speaks Spanish, while you always speak English.

Having simple conversations

There is also a lot you can do to enhance language development generally. For instance, when your toddler attempts a word or two-word sentence, repeat it back to him to reinforce what he is trying to say. If he says "Cat gone", you can say, "Yes, the cat is gone. Where has the cat gone?" Keep the sentences simple. By doing this you reiterate his attempts so he can hear what he is trying

to say more correctly, and you are also continuing the conversation and introducing new ideas and concepts that he can build on. Do not overtly "correct" his speech, as this can inhibit him speaking.

To keep a conversation going with your toddler, point things out to him, listen to and acknowledge what he might try to say, and reinforce his efforts. When you are dressing him, talk about the clothes he is putting on, and name body parts. When you are shopping in the supermarket, talk to him and describe what you are doing. Although it feels a bit odd at first to have what are sometimes one-way conversations, dialogue will build rapidly and be fun for both you and your child.

Using rhymes and songs

Nursery rhymes and songs help fill the gap, and are also great for developing language skills. Some even have hand gestures, which help your toddler remember words and their sequences within a song or rhyme. They also help your child to focus, because with repetition comes a sense of anticipation, waiting for what comes next, which helps him learn to concentrate for longer on one thing.

Reading together

Reading to your toddler is an activity that many family members can take part in and is a role most grandparents particularly enjoy. It provides a great way to bond with your toddler.

Looking at books with your toddler is also a good way of developing language. To look at a book together, you have to sit close or have your child on your lap. This type of one-to-one time creates a good opportunity for language learning, and it is greatly enhanced by your attentiveness and closeness.

In addition, reading a book out loud means that your child has to listen to enjoy the story and, because it is an enjoyable and rewarding situation, he will do so.

Choose picture books with attractive illustrations and clear story lines written for toddlers. If you are unsure which books to choose, ask your local children's librarian or children's bookseller for advice. And be guided by your toddler – let him choose the book he wants. A book is something that he will be happy to return to time and time again, so you will get a lot of use out of each one.

Books follow a sequence of events with which your child will become familiar. He will learn to anticipate events in a favourite storybook that you have read to him several times before. He will also be able to respond to your questions about events in the story, and will point at pictures if you ask him about them.

Safety

As your toddler becomes more mobile and explorative, she needs constant supervision and you may need to reconsider safety measures. Never underestimate how quickly she can move once your back is turned, or how far she can reach.

In the home

Be especially careful with hot drinks: a pot of freshly made tea or coffee is hot enough to scald and scar a young child badly. Always put them to the back of a work surface or table. Use the back rings of the cooker when cooking, and don't underestimate the heat of the outside of an oven door – keep your child well clear. Keep electrical flexes out of reach, and make it a habit to turn off socket switches when not in use. Electrical socket covers are also a useful precaution.

Stair-gates deter your child climbing, but it is also worth teaching your child how to go up and down the stairs safely with you. Avoid rugs that can be tripped over. Small items, such as buttons, coins, and rings, present a choking hazard, so ensure they are out of reach. Move houseplants out of reach, too, as some can be poisonous.

Glass-topped tables, French windows or doors should be made of safety glass or covered with safety film. Fit childproof catches to any doors and cover guards to tables. Make sure cleaning materials, medicines, and sharp objects are not accessible.

Out and about

When out and about with your child, make sure that she is securely strapped in her buggy, and don't carry so much on the handles it could topple over with her in it. Car seats must meet safety standards, be correctly installed, and used for all journeys. Car doors usually have the option of child locking as standard.

You must be extremely vigilant with toddlers around water – children can drown in just a few centimetres of water. You also should begin teaching your toddler what is and isn't safe, without instilling unnecessary fear. Explain why you insist on certain rules and behaviour.

DANGEROUS HEAT
Avoid doing the ironing with your toddler in the room. An iron can cause serious burns to an inquisitive toddler, who will manage to grab it if her mother turns her back for a minute.

How toddlers learn

Toddlers need plenty of opportunities to play with toys plus lots of interaction with other children and attentive adults. What looks like the unstructured chaos of toddler play is actually the basis of learning. Your toddler will use these playtimes to develop her physical, emotional, and cognitive abilities through exploration.

How toddlers learn skills

By the beginning of the second year, your baby will have developed a wealth of skills on which to build new ones. He has progressed from being a small baby, dependent on you to meet all his needs, to a very definite personality in his own right, with new and emerging physical, cognitive, and emotional skills.

Where initially your baby's skills were geared to basic survival, now they are enabling him to explore and expand his world with your help. By the age of 24 months, your toddler will have more in common with an adult than with his newborn self in terms of abilities.

Increased mobility

This period is one of increased mobility for your baby. It is about exploring further afield through a newly developed ability to move from A to B. Initially this may be through crawling, but it also occurs through learning to walk upright, which enables greater movement and also frees up the hands. Once a skill like walking has been learned then progress is about becoming more adept at doing it. Part of your child's playing is the doing of something over and over again to become better at it.

As your child becomes more proficient at moving around, he is able to see things in context and develop his spatial skills further. For example, it's hard to imagine a chair in context unless you can move around it. Also, if your toy rolls behind a chair, and you can get to it, you learn that when things disappear from view they don't actually disappear altogether. This is part of a learning process that the psychologists call "object permanence", meaning that something continues to exist, even after you can no longer see it.

During your baby's second year he is using all his senses to gain in experience and understanding of his world. Physical skills are greatly increased through mobility, and mobility is increased through the development and practice of physical skills. As a consequence, your toddler's cognitive, or learning, skills are influenced by his new view of the world. And emotional development moves ahead as your child utilizes these new skills to interact with others, and learns to become more social.

Communication skills

The other great area of development during this time is in communication skills and language development. Comprehension, and a developing understanding of the meaning of what you are saying, comes long before the first words are spoken. It is not until the meaning of a word is understood that the spoken word follows, which is why repetition is so important. As you do something, constantly speak to your toddler, telling him what you are doing. Eventually it becomes clear that your child understands simple words through his response to what you say. Long before he can say "shoes", he will help you look for his shoes when you ask him, for example.

Individuality

The rate of your baby's development depends partly on opportunities provided to develop different skills, but also on the inclination and individuality of your child. Some babies love to sit and focus on one thing for a time, absorbed in something quite stationary, while others are always on the go and keen to get up and about. Some will manage to get to where they want through crawling, and show no inclination to walk, while others may spend a short time bottom-shuffling before moving swiftly to walking.

PHYSICAL COORDINATION
This 18-month-old toddler has no difficulty getting down from the bed while holding a towel over his head!

1–2 years: your toddler's milestones

Your baby's milestones during the next 12 months are an important indicator of his developmental progress. Although all children are individual, there are a number of achievements that you can expect of your child during this year.

Movement milestones
- learns to walk unsupported
- walks, stops, and turns
- carries something in his hand while walking
- climbs safely on to a chair

Hand and finger milestones
- self-feeds with a spoon
- graduates from a feeder beaker to a cup
- throws an object, even if not in a straight line
- rotates wrist to unscrew an item

Social and emotional milestones
- learns to be happily apart from you for longer periods
- plays alongside another child
- shows loving behaviour to a toy, pet, or another child
- may help you with simple tasks

Language milestones
- progresses from single words to two-word utterances
- responds verbally to questions you ask
- enjoys naming everyday objects when he sees them

Intellectual skills
- remembers simple events that occur regularly
- makes connections between live objects and pictures
- begins to understand the concept of possession

12 to 14 months

Your baby's increasing ability to interact with her world is becoming more and more evident now. She will take every opportunity to explore as she is developing physical and cognitive skills. Her newfound ability to move around her environment will help with this, sometimes bringing her wishes into conflict with yours! Provide a safe place where she gets the chance to explore her abilities.

Physical development

By now your baby will have been able to sit securely for some time. She has probably been standing too, either holding on to you or another person, or a piece of furniture. She may already have taken her first steps, either cruising from one object or person to another, or taken her first steps alone. Almost half of all babies learn to walk at around this time, although many will still topple over if they lose momentum. But, if your baby has been walking since 10 months, or doesn't bother for another six months, that is normal too.

Provide lots of opportunities to use and strengthen the leg muscles in preparation for walking. Start by holding her hands as she practises taking her body weight on her feet while taking a few tentative steps. Babies' heads are big, in comparison to their bodies, and heavy. Until the legs strengthen, balance is a little unsteady as a consequence. What she will do when she begins to walk, however, is to walk with feet wide apart, toes pointing out, to give herself as broad a base as possible to improve her balance.

Fine motor skills

Your baby's fine motor skills are also improving through practice. Learning to let go of something provides quite a dramatic shift in ability, and brings together a number of skills. Before, if you gave your baby an object, she would tend to clasp it and hold on to it until she dropped it accidentally, or had it taken from her. This was because of the reflex to hold on that she was born with. Initially so strong, this ability to cling so tightly diminishes over the months. Now, at the age of about 12 months, she is reaching out, placing her hand over the object, deliberately picking it up, moving it to another place, and letting it go.

Hand movements are becoming more sophisticated. Your baby is beginning to turn her wrist in order to place an object more specifically into the place she wants it to go. This movement is a bit haphazard at first, as the physical development of the bones, which allows for greater manipulation, occurs over the first few years, just as the child is growing in maturity and dexterity. All this picking up and dropping of things – maddening though it can be – is part of the activity needed to practise these movements.

Your baby now begins to stretch her fingers out into the right position to pick something up in preparation – she is anticipating what she intends to do. She will also stretch out her arm towards something that she wants, to convey to you what it is.

Learning to walk

When babies are learning to walk, it is much more useful for them to learn with bare feet. A baby can tell a lot about the surface on which she is walking through what she can feel through the soles of her feet – whether the surface she is trying to walk on is smooth and soft, or hard and lumpy.

Don't be tempted to encase your toddler's feet in anything but the softest-soled shoes, and allow lots of opportunity for safe barefoot exploration. It is essential that you get your toddler's feet measured for length and width to ensure that the shoes you choose fit correctly. Your toddler will only need properly soled shoes when walking outside, and you will probably notice that walking with feet encased in shoes demands a slight adjustment at first, when your toddler may seem to walk less well initially. Hard, unyielding soles do little to help.

Cognitive development

With the right balance of stimulation and time to assimilate new experiences, babies' cognitive development starts to move forward in leaps and bounds now, building on everything that has been absorbed over the first year.

Verbal development

Your baby's first words are evidence of her cognitive development, and the beginning of an amazing new stage where communication extends into verbal language. And, as babies continue to watch what happens around them, they learn that objects have functions. You may now see your baby using a toy telephone like a real one: picking it up, putting it to the ear and putting it down. Soon she will be saying hello – or an approximation of the word – into the mouthpiece, and appearing to wait. She may not understand what the purpose of the telephone is at first, but it will soon start making sense to her when you put her ear to the real phone to listen to someone at the other end. It is as if small pieces of the jigsaw puzzle are being accumulated before she is able to make sense of the overall picture.

A sense of touch

We are all born with a sense of touch, but its development is dependent on having the experience of touching and feeling things.

Our ability to distinguish between different textures comes from our experience of feeling them. Touching an object to see what it feels like also provides a baby or toddler with the opportunity to use her hands in a different way, not to manipulate an object but to find out something about it. She can learn to explore and experiment by touching different substances and textures, such as water or fabrics.

Emotional development

Every baby is individual with a unique personality. Ensuring that all the physical needs of your baby are met really helps a baby's emotional development at this stage. It's hard to concentrate on learning to walk, or to deal with new people in your life, if you are tired and cranky, or

Toy box

Stacking toys

These provide an opportunity to learn about sizes, and how things fit together. Playing with stacking toys like blocks also involves using the hand to pick up and put down. Show her how to stack two blocks, one on top of the other, and she will try to copy you. At first she will probably only manage two blocks – one on top of the other – but with playful practice she will soon progress to stacking three and four blocks at a time without any difficulty at all.

Push-down/pop-up toys

While such toys rely on hand–eye coordination, they also help your child learn about cause and effect. When I do this – push down – then this happens – it pops up. It engages her attention because she is learning that one event leads to another, but doesn't yet know for sure that it will happen every time. Show her how it works, then let her make her own efforts. Is it easier to push down with the whole hand, or just one finger?

Textured toys

Use a variety of textured items – egg boxes, joining bricks, shiny paper, crinkly fabric, soft toys – and allow your child to explore their different properties, while you supervise. Do they scrunch up, are they smooth to touch, do they stick together?

hungry. Whenever possible, plan new activities or experiences for your baby when she is well rested, to ensure that an enjoyable time is had by both of you.

By now, close attachments have also been formed to a parent, a caregiver, and other close family members. Often there is a specially close attachment to one or two persons if there is a parent and childminder sharing the daily care. It is within this secure emotional environment that babies continue their development and learning.

Developing a love of reading

Books provide a focus for a quieter time, allowing your child to begin enjoying the pleasure of stories and imagination. Fictional stories explore ideas that help your child learn about what happens next and how characters react to events. They also provide the first steps towards learning to read, which happens within the shared or solitary enjoyment of looking at books.

Enjoying stories

At this stage books are not about learning to read – they are about enjoying stories for their own sake, and learning to focus and listen, both of which are important skills for the future. But books are also for sheer entertainment and the joy of returning to old favourites, books to be read time and time again, which in turn creates security.

★ You will have to show your baby how to look at and take care of books. Choose sturdy, wipeable board books at first. Their pages are easier for little fingers to turn. Keep your baby's books somewhere that is easy for your baby to get at, so she can choose them on her own.

★ Look at them together, with you reading the words. Explain things more fully as they come up in the story, while you have your toddler's focus and attention, and take time to discuss the pictures. This process also provides a time for closeness between the two of you, and can be usefully done at any time of the day for its own sake or for a quietening-down period, perhaps before bed.

★ Make sure there is no background noise when you are reading to your baby. Turn off the television, stereo, or radio, so that it is possible for her to really focus on listening to your voice as you read the words or for you to answer her questions about the story or pictures.

1 Sit with your baby held closely in your lap. Hold the book open so he can see the pictures clearly, and begin reading. Give your baby plenty of time to look at each page.

2 Respond to your baby's reactions to the pictures or the story. Enjoy his enjoyment in the tale, or the surprises the book contains.

14 to 16 months

Once your baby starts walking, you may find that his explorer instincts open up a whole new world as you adjust to this new phase. Create a safe place for him to play, which allows exploration within a safe and secure environment. He is not being naughty, but his instinct to explore is stronger than his memory of what you've told him about not touching the electric socket!

Physical development

By now, if your child has learned to walk he will be getting steadier on his feet and can begin to walk – although slowly – longer distances. What he will probably also do is to rely quite strongly on using his arms for balance, occasionally holding on to you or to pieces of furniture as he makes progress. And, as he walks alone, his arms are held away from his body on each side to help him balance when standing alone. Instead of toppling over, he will probably sit down quite deliberately if he feels he is losing his balance.

Handedness

At this age your toddler will probably use both hands equally. Some toddlers may begin to show a preference for using either the right or left hand when playing, feeding, or drinking from a cup, but most children do not consistently use one hand rather than another until they reach about three years old.

The hand a child shows preference for is genetically determined. If both parents are right-handed, there is a 98 per cent chance of their child being so, too. When one parent is left-handed, there is a 17 per cent chance of a child being left-handed, and where both parents are left-handed, this increases to 50 per cent.

Advances in self-feeding

Being able to grasp an object has made self-feeding possible for some time, although being unable to turn the spoon into the mouth has, at first, made this a bit haphazard. As your child is more able to twist her wrist and turn the spoon towards her mouth, this gets easier.

Being able to drink from a cup also becomes easier for the same reason – bringing the beaker to the mouth then being able to turn it towards the mouth becomes more possible as this twisting movement improves.

Play activities that help develop this ability will also help your toddler achieve other skills that make her more independent.

Don't try to influence deliberately which hand your toddler uses: he will use the one that feels most natural to him.

Fine motor skills

Fine motor skills, smaller movements of the hands, are developing, along with hand–eye coordination. At first, toddlers tend to point with their finger, hand, and whole arm when they want something, but over time they learn just to use the finger to communicate their wishes to you.

Building bricks can be used in a variety of ways to help your child develop his fine motor skills. You can count them and group them as well as build with them. No doubt, when you play with him, most of the fun for your toddler is in knocking the bricks down that you have carefully stacked. But introducing the idea of balance to him by showing him how to build bricks is laying good foundations. The first time he manages to place one block on top of another is quite an achievement.

Cognitive development

Your child's attention span is beginning to lengthen and, if he isn't distracted by feeling tired, thirsty, or hungry, he can focus on an activity for a little longer. This is because he is beginning to develop memory, through repeated activity, so he is beginning to anticipate the pleasure of a book when you suggest it, for example, or going for a walk, or having a bath. And during an activity, if he is distracted for a moment and discontinues it, he will return to what he was doing after a pause.

Through the daily routine, your child develops an understanding of what might happen next. This understanding can then begin to be transferred to other events.

Verbal skills

At this stage your child will probably be saying, or attempting to say, a few words. Children vary enormously: some will say nothing at all for months then come out with a three-word sentence, while others will attempt to say individual words, however inaccurately, until they make themselves understood. Often a child will begin with one word, such as "dog" or "daddy", but apply it to all animals or to all men.

Emotional development

Babies who are cherished, cuddled, and kissed learn, by example, how to pass on similar expressions of positive emotion to others, and you may also see this extended to their toys. Equally, expressions of dissatisfaction may be displayed. Your toddler may get angry at a toy, but it doesn't usually last for long. Young children are often very responsive to the emotional environment in which they live. They may not understand it but they often pick up on your happiness or sadness – laughing with you, or stroking your face if you are sad.

The role of soft toys

A favourite toy, to which a child can form an attachment, can help some children make the transition from your company to being happily alone. It can become a "transitional object". Many young children find the presence of a familiar toy at bedtime quite reassuring.

Soft toys can also help develop a child's imagination, as they give their toy characteristics, or act out happy or sad times with it. They can also use their soft toys to act out feelings. Talking to your toddler about feelings through a favourite soft toy can help him learn how to empathize. Does she look sad? Why does she look sad? How can we make her feel happy?

You could get more than one of a favourite toy or blanket. Then, if the first one is lost or becomes worn out, it can be replaced by another that is exactly like it.

Toy box

Push–along toys

Pushing something along can be done for its own sake, or it can be incorporated into early, imaginative play – for example, putting a favourite soft toy into a miniature stroller or buggy, and taking it "for a walk".

★ A toy wheelbarrow in which things can be carried elsewhere is also fun, as is a toy vacuum cleaner that can be used alongside an adult using the real thing!

★ Some push-along toys are designed to make a musical noise when used, while others may include a dog on wheels (which incorporates the pleasure of a soft toy into imaginative play).

★ Some push-along trolleys come complete with a set of building bricks, which provide extra fun in being loaded and unloaded, and can be used to build towers.

Water play

Water play really begins from birth, when your baby enjoys his first bath. Water is great fun to play with, and has lots of interesting properties that make it useful for exploration. Just pouring water from one plastic beaker into another helps your child develop hand–eye coordination.

Bath and basin games

Provide a variety of different-sized plastic containers, even a plastic tea set with small teapot, which challenges coordination further when trying to pour from the spout. Playing somewhere where spills don't matter helps your toddler gain in confidence, as does helping to clear up a spill if it happens.

★ Lots of bath toys provide opportunities for pouring, while some also include other possibilities like turning a tap to allow water through or not.

★ Water play introduces the idea of different weights, a beaker of water feels heavier than an empty one, and provides opportunities to learn about other properties of water – for example, it always flows down and not up – and here you have the beginnings of understanding about why the rain falls down and rivers don't run uphill. Your toddler can also learn, through play, about the things that float, such as lolly sticks made of wood, and those that sink, such as a pebble.

★ The important bit is the fun and enjoyment your child gets out of learning about water, or the imaginative play about boats crossing the sea, but this sort of play is also making a contribution to a wider understanding of how the world works.

Paddling-pool play

Water play can be extended from basins and baths into paddling pools, where your toddler will learn to feel comfortable sharing space with other children, getting splashed, and participating in the rough and tumble of communal play. The confidence in water that this develops paves the way towards feeling confident in a swimming pool and, eventually, towards the confidence that precedes learning to swim.

★ Whenever your toddler is playing around in even a shallow pool, you need to provide constant supervision to avoid the risk of drowning accidents.

BASIN PLAY
This child is really enjoying playing with water in his own garden. He discovers that leaves float – unless you push them down – and that you can create exciting splashes by simply waving your hand about in the water.

16 to 18 months

Now that your toddler can concentrate for longer periods of time, she may get totally absorbed in playing a particular game – a developmental milestone for her. Don't expect her to take kindly to being told to finish off a game without adequate warning! Even then, she will need reassurance that she can play the same game again another time – and soon!

Physical development

With her walking skills getting better and better, and with her arms free, it now becomes possible to pick up and carry an object while walking. This usually requires two hands, so balance has to have improved enough not to need the arms for balancing. Being able to walk, and stand securely, also opens up the possibility of reaching for objects that were previously out of reach.

Don't underestimate how far a toddler can reach: make sure objects are placed far enough away to be out of danger. It's all too easy for a toddler to grab a hot cup of coffee left too close to the edge of a table. Accidents often happen because your child has made something of a developmental leap and you have not quite caught up with her.

Playing outdoors

Using their bodies in an energetic and expressive way helps children develop balance, coordination and strength, and much of this sort of play needs to be done outdoors. Make sure that your child wears suitable clothing when playing outdoors – clothes that you won't mind getting muddy or crumpled, and that won't catch when your child is trying to negotiate a slide with your help.

Learning to be adventurous on swings and slides doesn't come naturally to every child, and yours might need some encouragement. But when she sees other children having a go, and having fun, then this can encourage her too. This sort of play, if there are other children around, also helps her to learn about taking turns and taking care.

Take your toddler to the playground in your local park or to an indoor soft-play facility. In addition to pushing her on the baby swings, let her try out the small slides and mini climbing frames. Both will help her develop her hand–eye coordination as well as provide her with exercise and plenty of fun. She may well team up with another toddler of similar age, and they will chase each other excitedly around the playground.

Outdoor play can also include first games with balls. Choose a medium-size ball a bit smaller than a football and much lighter, so it won't knock your toddler over if thrown too hard, and your toddler can hold it in two hands. At first there will be very little hand–eye coordination, which is what makes actually catching a ball possible. This takes a lot of practice. But for now it is worth introducing the idea, and making a game of throwing, rolling, and catching balls outside.

Learning to throw

Once your toddler has learned how to let go, the next possibility is throwing. Although first attempts demonstrate that toddlers cannot throw with any accuracy, this will improve with practice. Give your toddler scrunched-up paper balls or soft foam balls to throw. Keep heavy objects out of reach of your toddler.

Cognitive development

By this stage your toddler's understanding has increased to the point of carrying out simple requests like "Give me the cup." Single requests are within her ability, but if you ask her to put down her book, fetch her shoes, and close the door, this would be beyond her ability because it requires her to remember a sequence of events in order. She would probably be able to do all three things, if you asked her to do them one at a time.

Your toddler's developing language may still be limited to one word at a time, but voiced in a different tone to convey different meaning. "Dadda!" might mean "Come here!" while "Dadda?", as she holds out a toy, might suggest "Help me." And "Dadda" said while pointing at a cup, might mean "I want a drink". Soon two-word sentences begin, so you might hear "Dadda, here!" or "Dadda, please?" or "Dadda, drink." Reinforce what you hear by asking, "Would you like a drink?" This way, you let her know you've understood her request, and help her to understand how to say things correctly.

Learning responsibility

At the end of a play session encourage your toddler to put the toys back into the box. At this age, doing this is just as much of a game as anything else, and if it is presented as such it starts to pave the way towards caring for things and putting them away after using them. We call it tidying up, and presume our child will find it boring – don't make that assumption and they won't either! Don't refer to it as "helping me", either; it's a game and one she wants to play if you make it interesting, talking all the time – "Here's the red one. Can you find the green one for me?", "And… put it in the box! Now it's my turn." This will help her learn to value and take care of her possessions.

Emotional development

One change you may now notice is that your toddler will begin to recognize what pleases and what annoys you, and she may try out different behaviours to see what your reaction is. This is an extension of her learning about how she can influence her world, and is a way in which she learns to engage your attention. It is best simply to ignore any behaviours that displease you, so that she does not gain attention from doing them.

At this stage, she will want to please you, so it's worth encouraging good behaviour by giving her lots of attention when she behaves in a way that does please you.

Constructive scribbling

Making your mark permanent, even if it's just a streak of purple on a white page, is quite a thrill when done for the first time. It is very clear evidence that you can make something happen! And if this is joined by other colours, and eventually celebrated and pinned to the wall like a "proper" picture, it is a very rewarding process for a toddler.

Paper and crayons

First scribbles are very important – they are early expressions of creativity. Provide lots of paper – it doesn't have to be new; the back of junk mail is good, or discarded computer print-outs – and half a dozen colourful, thick wax crayons that are easy to grip for small fingers, in an easily accessible container for your child. You will need to make it clear that only paper should be drawn on, but if yours is a particularly expressive and experimental child then other surfaces may be considered fair game at first. You can quite see why a nice white wall might be thought suitable, so you will need to be very clear about what's OK and what's not.

★ First scribbles are very important. They give her an idea of what she can achieve and, over time, using crayons in this way helps her learn to control the movements of her hand. Using the thicker wax crayons, allow your toddler to experiment with her own ways of holding the crayon when scribbling. It is best to wait until she is two years old before encouraging her

Becoming independent

You may also find that your toddler is quite happy to be independent of you in a group, occasionally checking to see that you are available to her if she needs you. Sometimes, however, in new situations, the need for reassurance is temporarily increased. You may find a period of clinginess arises, as a new adaptation is needed. This is normal behaviour while getting used to a new situation. Give your toddler the reassurance she needs, but don't become overprotective: it will pass.

Toy box

Building blocks

Building blocks that fit together take the possibilities of building blocks a little further. They require a bit more in the way of deliberate coordination, as the fit needs to be a little more accurate, and it takes more strength to push them together. But the rewards are greater, as the blocks stay together.

Playing with building blocks that fit together is great for boys and girls. With a little prompting from you, they will soon learn to use their imaginations to build a house, or a garage, or just put the colours together in particular patterns.

Activity toys

Activity centres or activity boards combine a variety of pushing, pulling, turning, and twisting movements that illustrate cause and effect. The reward for your toddler is the result but, along the way, she has developed her hand–eye coordination. This will also improve her skill with a spoon when self-feeding.

to hold a crayon in the proper way. Movements are large at first, covering wide areas of the paper, and become smaller later as her fine motor control – the small movements she needs to make in order to manage writing later on – improves.

★ Scribbling with crayons allows your toddler to practise twisting and turning movements of the hand. Her hand–eye coordination, as well as fine motor control, need to come together to do this. Encourage your toddler to have fun, enjoying the patterns she makes, so that she wants to continue to make more scribbles.

★ Don't concern yourself with which hand she chooses to use for drawing at this stage, as she may use both equally before she opts more and more for one rather than the other.

EXPRESSING CREATIVITY
Mum and toddler share some creative time while drawing, scribbling, and using imagination. This toddler makes a bold squiggly line right across the blue paper. He shows good hand control in his ability to make individual lines. His mother joins in the fun, choosing a blue pen to draw with. She encourages him to make more of his own lines with his orange pen. By doing this, he is further developing his hand–eye coordination.

18 to 20 months

Toddlers are naturally curious, and will learn to make important discoveries by themselves. If you constantly entertain your toddler, he won't develop his own ability to find things out for himself. Toddlers don't get bored if they have a good learning environment, even if they can't concentrate for very long yet, because their whole world is open to discovery.

Physical development

Your toddler may now be able to walk faster, and even run a little without stumbling, although children at this age vary considerably in what they can and want to achieve. If he is gently chased when playing, your toddler can speed up quite considerably and will also do so if excited. The large muscle groups in the legs have become much stronger through use, and give your child more control over stopping and starting when he is walking.

His movements are much more controlled generally, and may now include taking backwards and sideways steps. What also becomes possible now, with better balance and greater strength in the legs, is a kicking movement. At first, standing on one leg momentarily can be destabilizing and it takes practice to become proficient at doing so and then kicking out. Accuracy will be poor at first and, instead of actually kicking the ball, your child may effectively stand on it, which won't achieve his objective – yet!

Smaller movements

Because your child's fine motor skills are improving, he is more able to grasp a small object using his thumb and forefinger. This makes much smaller movements – such as undoing a large zip fastener – possible, although it may take some concentration and effort at first, and some children of this age will not be quite able to do it on their own.

All those activities that encourage pressing knobs, turning switches, and twisting handles, have helped, and now it is much easier for him to attempt something like posting a shape through its matching hole. Accuracy is improving all the time through playing, which practises these skills, and being able to achieve tasks independently – such as drinking regularly from a cup – all demonstrate his bringing together of motor skills.

Cognitive development

By now your toddler will probably have a vocabulary of between 50 and 200 words. The development of memory and of language are closely linked, so you may be aware of a big leap in his general understanding of the way the world works as his speech improves. What he says is now becoming more sophisticated, too. Whereas before it was more a question of naming objects – dog, car, shoe – or linking an adjective with an object – a red bus – now he may be using abstract concepts. He may also show that he is beginning

Sorting out shapes

A shape sorter, in which different-shaped objects must be matched to the same shapes in the side of a box, provides an extremely good opportunity for your toddler to enjoy developing spatial awareness and hand control. The shape has to be correctly matched, lined up, and pushed through.

Initially, this will be quite difficult for him to do, and you may have to line the piece up for him at first to demonstrate, allowing him to push it through. In order for him to want to try it needs to be rewarding, and over time, when it has become possible, he will return to the game again and again.

to understand that objects belong to people; for example, "my doll".

You may see how far your toddler's understanding has progressed when you make a complicated request to him, such as "Please go to the hall and get me your shoes." If he is able to do this, then he has understood a number of things – he has to remember where the hall is and how to find it, go there, find the right shoes from the rack, get them, and bring them back to you. This is a big leap in his cognitive skills.

Learning from books

By now your toddler will probably have quite a good selection of books, and visiting the local library to choose and borrow books is another activity that can be routinely enjoyed by you and your toddler. Have a

Musical activities

An appreciation of music can, in itself, be life-enriching for your toddler, and you may already share music with him by singing and dancing together at home. Musical toys can contribute to this enjoyment, and first toys – like a simple xylophone – can give enormous pleasure.

Sounding notes

Hand-eye coordination is required to hit the keys of a xylophone with the stick, and at first this will be a haphazard affair. But it does demonstrate cause and effect, and the possibility of influencing your environment through choice. The different keys provide different notes, and hitting them in a variety of sequences creates a range of musical effects. Don't expect a tune, though: this is about exploring noise! This activity will interest and absorb him as he listens to the sounds he produces, and listening skills are always worth practising.

Beating a rhythm

Other musical toys, such as a drum, tambourine, or hand-held bells, also produce noises, and allow your child to explore rhythm. Learning about rhythm, even indirectly, can be the beginning of learning how to keep to a rhythm, which is useful for other physical skills like dancing.

Identifying and copying a beat can be quite sophisticated, but it can also be very simple – 1, 2, 3, for example. You can copy the beat of a nursery rhyme – "Pat-a-cake, Pat-a-cake" – for example. Or you can pick out the beat of the syllables of your name – "Ti-mo-thy", for example, is 1, 2, 3.

You can also make simple, homemade shakers – a handful of uncooked rice or macaroni in a sealed plastic bottle makes a pleasant noise. And your toddler can use one of these while dancing to music or singing a song, picking out the rhythm with the shaker. This has the added benefit of allowing several children to participate, helping concentration and collaboration and promoting the idea of a joint activity.

MAKING MUSIC
These two toddlers are having great fun sounding notes on their instruments. They listen to the different sounds attentively and with pleasure.

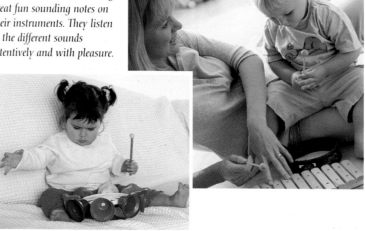

special shelf or book box where you keep your child's books and where he can get them for himself. And always keep a favourite book in your bag when you are out and about, as it will give your toddler something to look at and talk about if you are waiting somewhere.

Find time at least once a day to sit and read stories to your toddler. This quiet, absorbing activity will give you some peaceful, restorative time together. If you have more than one child of differing ages, try reading one story to all of them at the same time. Ask them each to choose a story, and read each story in turn. This will also help them to learn about taking turns and patience.

Having stories read aloud encourages imagination and helps your toddler learn to focus on your voice while having fun. Talk around the stories you read, asking questions about the pictures, as well as reading the words. Always take your cue from your child: some children hate it if you deviate from the written word, as they love the rhythm and familiarity of a favourite story. With very simple picture books, even at this early age your toddler will probably start to memorize some of the words he sees written down. This early understanding of books and the written word will help him later on when he starts learning to read.

Toy box

Modelling clay

Making shapes out of soft, pliable, coloured dough can give your toddler hours of creative play. Clear a space on the kitchen table and show him how to roll the dough with his fingers to make sausage shapes. He could also have fun making flat shapes, using a child's rolling pin and some plastic pastry cutters or shape moulds.

Sand play

Sand has all sorts of interesting properties that can be explored. It trickles through the fingers or a toy. It feels gritty, and sticks to your hands. If you put a lot of sand into a large container, it gets heavy. If you make sand wet, it sticks together and will keep the shape of another object. Sand can mean hours of exploratory fun, alone or with an adult or another child. It also means using your hands in different ways, and using tools, which helps develop manual dexterity. Adult supervision is always necessary, as there is a risk of sand getting in toddlers' eyes.

If you have a garden, it's worth having a sandpit. Sand must be fine and washed. Any sandpit needs a lid, or cats and dogs will treat it as a litter tray (cat faeces can contain the toxicaris worm, which can be dangerous to your child's health).

You will need a selection of plastic containers or buckets to play with, and other plastic toys: hand spades, a sieve, a miniature broom or brush, shape moulds and cutters, and plastic cars or animals.

Emotional development

Although your toddler might begin to understand about an object belonging to him, at this stage of his development he is unlikely to get too upset if it is snatched away from him. Unless he has an emotional dependency on a favourite toy, he is more likely simply to reach for another toy to play with and continue his game. His interactions with other children are limited and, although he will enjoy being around other children of similar age, any playing he does is in parallel rather than interacting with them.

By this stage, he may smile at other children of all ages, and like to watch what they are doing and imitate them, especially if they are a bit older.

20 to 22 months

Even though your toddler is becoming increasingly independent, sometimes she attempts more than she can manage. Offer the help she needs rather than taking over completely, and praise her efforts even if she does not quite complete the task. The more she is able to manage by herself, the more her self-esteem will grow, and the happier she will be.

Physical development

By now walking, running, stopping, and starting movements are usually well coordinated and something you have begun to take for granted as your toddler becomes much more physically capable. Your toddler will also attempt to climb off and on objects, such as sofas and chairs, depending on how adventurous a personality she is, and perhaps even in and out of her cot or bed.

Climbing stairs will probably be attempted, on hands and knees. If you have stairs, teach your toddler to come downstairs backwards, on her hands and knees, from step to step, which is much safer than trying to come down facing forwards. If you are coming downstairs with her, she can walk down slowly, holding on to your hand.

Using her hands

Carrying something in her hands as she walks is probably routine now if it's not too large, and she may try to carry two items, one in each hand.

Her fine motor skills are now more developed, meaning that not only can she use her hands to greater effect, but she can also use tools more efficiently. This can range from digging in a sandpit with a shovel, to scribbling on paper and banging a drum. She may also try to do

those tasks that you have always done for her independently, such as trying to put on her waterproof boots by herself or doing up the simple buckles on her new shoes.

Cognitive development

By constantly building on what she already knows and understands, your toddler continues to extend her understanding of the world. Now, if she puts a cup on her head she knows that is not its proper use – although she may experiment with pretending it is a hat – and she is expressing her understanding of this through her game.

She often demonstrates her understanding of what happens next through her anticipation of it: for example, if you put on her coat, she may go and stand next to the door ready to go out. If you pass her a book upside down, she will turn it the right way up and sit down ready to read or be read to.

Games that she has played in one simple way before may be experimented with, and used in a different way to see what might happen. Posting shapes, for example, may have been done routinely in the past, but now she might pick up the box and look underneath to see where it has gone.

Pretend play

The development of imagination is helped enormously by encouraging pretend play. Pretend play usually begins through imitation – so, for example, when you played peekaboo you pretended you had gone away by hiding your face and reappearing, and your baby copied you. This extends into other activities. She has seen you drive the car, so she will sit and pretend to drive a car by

Ball play

Throwing balls accurately takes practice, as does kicking a ball, but it's possible for your toddler to have a go at this age. Balls are quite interesting in themselves because, unlike other things when dropped, they bounce. Ball play is also a good family activity.

Make sure that the ball used for kicking and throwing is not too heavy, and that your toddler has plenty of space to practise in – preferably outside.

turning an imaginary steering wheel and making the noise, "vroom, vroom". She will pretend to pour tea from the toy teapot into a cup, and milk from a toy milk jug. Then she will put in sugar and stir it, before pretending to drink it. She remembers a sequence of events and pretends to do it as part of her game.

You may well be required to take part in pretend games, because you are given a plastic cup of pretend tea, and expected to "drink" it. All the time your toddler is playing these pretend games, she is beginning to understand the distinction between what's real and what's not.

Learning about nature

Playing outdoors gives a child the opportunity to experience the natural world. It's very different from playing indoors, with all its restrictions, and being outdoors makes it possible to try out new activities, such as playing with a ball, jumping in puddles, or running without any hindrance or worry.

It's also difficult to be aware of the weather when indoors – but when you are outdoors you can feel the wind and see its effect on the trees, for example. Walking in the countryside or a park also gives an opportunity to look at leaves, and other growing things, and also to see older children riding bikes, or scooters, or skateboards.

Talk about the leaves on the trees, the seasons of the year, how the temperature changes influence how things grow. Keep it simple, but point things out and name them. All of this will help her observation skills and her vocabulary. You can also point out things like the reflections in puddles and the shapes made by clouds in the sky, plus why we have a shadow that moves with us. All of this helps instil an appreciation and enjoyment of the environment in which we live.

Emotional development

Learning to think about others takes a long time, and can only follow self-awareness. As your toddler becomes more self-aware, physically and then emotionally, she can extend her feelings about herself to others. This starts with those who are closest to her, which is why you may see some evidence of this

Toy box

Tray puzzles

Matching shapes in tray puzzles is a development of shape-sorting, and a precursor to simple jigsaw puzzles. It is all about identifying and matching shapes. You may have to show your child what is expected of her before encouraging her to have a go.

★ Tip out the pieces and show her how you look at the piece and find the matching shape on the board; show her how you may have to move the shape around to make it match. Place the shape by its home so she can see how it matches up before putting it in place. Take your cue from your toddler. Some children welcome help, while others can't bear it and want to work it out for themselves.

★ Tray puzzles help train the eye and develop the ability to match shapes. This is a valuable skill for later on, when your child begins to identify letters through their shapes, and also words – the word "elephant" has quite a recognizable shape! Matching shapes does, eventually, help your child when it comes to learning to read and write.

in her relationship with you – on whom she is still so dependent – but not necessarily with others.

Close family members can create the emotional security that allows your toddler to consider the feelings of other people, as long as her attention is drawn to them. For example, if you point out that an older child is upset, your toddler may express sympathy by giving the child a hug and a kiss. Empathy – the ability to feel as the other person does – comes from experience, which takes time, so don't expect it yet!

Fun with painting

Your child can use paints in a variety of ways without using a brush – she simply needs hands and feet! You need thick water-based paint, and the three primary colours – red, yellow, and blue. You can experiment with one colour at a time, or by mixing two to make a third, or using them all together to make a gungy brown, which begins the exploration of the different properties of colour.

Finger painting

Finger painting is deliciously messy and very tactile, and gives your child a real hands-on experience of making her mark. You will probably need several sheets of paper to experiment with different effects.

Hand prints

Hand prints require a slightly different technique, and possibly some adult help to paint one hand at a time, all over, and then to carefully press down. First attempts will be undoubtedly splodgy, but eventually they will provide an opportunity to talk about fingerprints and individuality.

Footprints

Footprints require adult help if you are to avoid paint being trodden elsewhere, especially as balancing alone on one foot isn't possible yet. Footprints make a unique record of your child's growth, and you can compare children's hand and foot sizes, talking about whose is bigger.

HANDS–ON EXPERIENCE
This toddler's mother helps him to paint thick dark-blue paint on to the palm of his left hand. Once his hand is thoroughly covered in paint, he spreads his fingers and presses his hand on the paper to make a print. She is helping him develop his own hand print, and he loves doing them!

22 to 24 months

Your toddler has become increasingly independent over the preceding 12 months, but he still needs your unconditional love and understanding. One feature of life with a toddler is a constant pulling away from and returning to parent or caregiver for support. Meeting a toddler's emotional needs means being constantly aware of his fluctuations, trying to understand him, and adapting to support him.

Physical development

The difference between the baby who couldn't walk just over a year ago, and the toddler who can now walk, run, and kick, demonstrates the amazing combination of physical skills that has led to these achievements over the second year.

Muscle coordination

Climbing off and on low furniture and on small climbing frames in the playground is probably routinely attempted and achieved. If you watch your toddler you can see that he is usually quite cautious, looking round to judge the distance and stretching one leg to find the ground and then the other. Some toddlers will also try to jump up and down, but their feet don't yet tend to leave the ground! All the time muscles are being strengthened and coordinated, and activities like kicking a ball become possible through practice.

Your toddler's ability to squat down and pick something up, then return easily to a standing position, is now quite proficient because of the increased strength and flexibility in his hip and knee joints. But his running may still be a little stiff, and he may still have insufficient strength and coordination to manage running around corners without slowing down.

Dexterous hands

Your toddler's hands are now much more dexterous.

★ She can manage smaller, manipulative movements, which makes her hands much more capable, using the whole hand to unscrew the lid of a jar, for example, or her finger and thumb to pick up something quite small.

★ She can use objects as tools more proficiently, or place things one on top of the other more specifically.

★ Fingers are used to point, poke, or prod – used singly or together – and your toddler can calculate how best to use her hands to achieve the result she wants.

Cognitive development

Physical experiences help to develop your toddler's cognitive skills. For example:

● Your child knows that the toy hammer is for banging with and would use this correctly now, instead of another toy.

● He knows that toy cars go "brrrrmmmm, brrrrmmmm" but a plastic cow goes "moooo".

● He can make connections between a toy car and the family car, a plastic cow and one in a book or in a field. He knows that each car has similar properties but that they are different: one is real, and the other is not.

And all the time he is talking about what he is seeing and learning, which means that you are reinforcing his knowledge with your questions or corrections in response. There is a massive shift in understanding as his language develops because of this, and because of his developing memory.

Language and memory

Memory and language are closely linked. It is much easier to remember something when it has a name than when it is just an abstract object. Make as much effort as you can to talk to and with your toddler, as this will help his cognitive development enormously. If you are reinforcing

Toy box

Crayons and paper

Having been introduced to the idea of crayons and paper at an earlier stage in his development, your child will probably want to scribble and draw regularly by now.

★ His hand movements are crude at first, but through his experimentation with colours and shapes he will learn that he can exert greater control over his movements and will gain in confidence with crayons.

★ Allow him to experiment with a variety of different crayons and felt pens (choose washable felt pens, in case of accidents). As he draws, tell him the colours and talk with him about what he is trying to express through his scribbles.

★ Don't assume that you can interpret what your child is trying to draw – let him tell you!

his efforts to communicate, it encourages him to go on trying. In addition, if you are repeating what he says and building on it, this helps. For example when he points and says, "Car", you can say, "Yes, that's your car. That's your blue car. Would you like to put your teddy in your blue car?" Not only are you responding to and reinforcing what he is saying, but you are giving him a lot more relevant information.

You are also helping him develop his ability to think about what to do next, which helps develop his imagination. On another occasion when he is playing with his car and

Imaginative play

Playing with first cars, trains, soft toys, and dolls, whether your child is a girl or a boy, provides them with opportunities for imaginative play. It also helps them to develop their own stories and events, which they can play out with these toys.

Playing with dolls and toy figures

You will probably find that your toddler concentrates quite hard while playing imaginatively with his toy figure or doll, and may talk about what is happening in his game, chattering away to himself.

★ Boys tend to talk less when they play with dolls or toy figures, as their games tend to include more action.

★ Both boys and girls will copy what they've seen happen in real life, and at this age will probably copy various parenting activities they have experienced in your company.

★ Your toddler may pretend to feed a doll, put it to bed, or give it a bath.

★ Looking after a sick dolly – giving pretend medicine, sticking a plaster on the knee, bandaging the arm – makes a great game.

★ Toys don't need to be sophisticated, either: an old shoebox and a tea towel make a very good bed and blanket for a teddy to sleep in.

★ Toddlers sometimes act out their own experiences with their dolls, helping to make sense of events in their daily lives.

Playing with cars

Both girls and boys enjoy playing with cars and trains.

★ At this age toddlers still tend to play alongside each other, although elements of social play are beginning to emerge. So sharing a group of cars may not work, but if each child has their own car they may happily play together, learning how to take turns. Look for opportunities to acknowledge and praise sharing, and "head off" any potential conflict before it occurs. Children need coaches not judges.

teddy, he will remember what you said. He will put the teddy in the car and move his language along, saying "Teddy in", for example. Then, over time, he may say "Teddy in car" or "Teddy in blue car".

Whenever you are with your toddler, whether playing, feeding, or putting on his shoes, talk to him and describe what you are doing, using lots of adjectives. Talk about putting on his brown shoes, one foot, then the other, and doing them up. Giving him a verbal description contributes to his understanding. Remember, too, to allow him time to respond to you, and the conversation will soon flow!

Using books

By now books will be part of your regular repertoire of resources. Although books are something that you can share with your child, also encourage him to use books on his own, perhaps suggesting that he looks at a book in bed while waiting for you to come and settle him at night, or when he is having a quiet time during the day.

In addition, start using books to look at pictures of something he has seen – an animal book after a visit to a zoo, for example. This gives you something to talk about and refer to, identifying the animals you have seen. In addition, it introduces your toddler to the idea of books as a source of information.

Emotional development

As your toddler experiences more of the world, and develops the language to talk about his experiences, he also begins to think about how he feels and how others feel. This may become apparent first of all through expressions of his own feelings – happiness, anger, sadness – which can be overwhelming and may be expressed in a tantrum.

Managing feelings

For now feelings can be expressed in a variety of ways, and learning how to manage them, especially in a group, is the beginning of your toddler becoming socially able.

Unwanted behaviour towards another child can be because of an inability to manage feelings, and you will want to help your toddler deal with these. But it is only through experiencing mixing with other children that it is possible to practise managing feelings in a group, and to become emotionally aware.

Always remember that a hungry, tired, bored, or overextended toddler is much more likely to exhibit unwanted behaviours.

CAR CITY
This toddler plays with his toy car. He moves the car around an imaginary world, commentating on the action as he enacts it.

Index

attention span, 45–6

balls, 49, 57
bedtime routines, 25–6
books, 35, 43, 54–5, 63
bottle-feeding, 27, 29
bowel movements, 20–1
breast-feeding, 27, 29
building blocks, 18, 19, 42, 45, 51

calming activities, 23
childcare, 11, 13, 43
choking, 28, 36
climbing, 57, 61
cognitive development, 42, 45–6, 49–50, 53–5, 57–8, 61–3
communication *see* language development
concentration, 14, 35
confrontation, avoiding, 15
crawling, 38
cruising, 41
crying, 27

developmental checks, 18–19
discipline, 14–15
dolls 62
drawing, 50–1, 62

dreams, 27
drinks, 29, 31, 45

eating habits, 30
emotional development, 10–11, 38, 42–3, 46, 50–1, 55, 58–9, 63
feeding, 28–31, 45
finger foods, 29
fruit juices, 29, 31
frustration, 16–17, 23

games, 22–3, 47, 57–8
gender differences, 22–3

hand control, 41, 45, 53, 57, 61
handedness, 45
health checks, 18–19
hearing, 18, 19, 33

illnesses, 19
imagination, 11, 57–8, 62–3
immunization, 19
independence, 17, 51

language development, 19, 32–5, 39, 42, 46, 50, 53–4, 61–3

mealtimes, 29
memory, 14, 46, 53, 61–2
milestones, 39

milk, 29
motor skills, 18, 41, 45, 51, 53, 57
muscle development, 41, 53, 61
music, 22, 23, 54

nappies, 20, 21
naps, 7, 19, 23, 24–6
nature, learning about, 58
night waking, 26–7
nursery rhymes, 35

outdoor play, 49, 58

painting, 59
personality, 39
physical development, 22–3, 38, 41, 45, 49, 53, 57, 61
play, 11, 22, 47, 49, 57–8
position in family, 9
potty-training, 20–1
pretend play, 57–8

reading, 23, 34, 35, 43, 55
responsibility, learning, 50
running, 61

safety, 36, 49
scribbling, 50–1, 62
security, 10–11, 17, 27, 59
self-feeding, 29, 45

self-image, 12
separation anxiety, 11
sharing, 13
shoes, 41
sibling relationships, 8–9, 12
sleep, 7, 19, 23, 24–7
smacking, 14
snacks, 23, 30
social development, 12–13
soft toys, 46
songs, 35
spatial skills, 38
speech *see* language development
stairs, 36, 57

talking *see* language development
tantrums, 16–17
teeth, 28, 30–1
television, 33
throwing, 49, 57
toilet training, 20–1
touch, sense of, 42
toys, 13, 42, 46, 51, 53, 55, 58, 62
twins, 9

verbal skills *see* language development

walking, 38, 41, 45, 49, 53
water play, 47

Acknowledgments

Credits

Jacket photo: Camille Tokerud/Getty Images
Jacket design: Nicola Powling
Indexer: Hilary Bird
Proof-reader: Nikky Twyman
Models: Lilian with Gregory Maya, Tracey with James Coleman-Ward, Faith Knight with her dad, Janis and Maureen Lopatkin with Mia Lopatkin, Mrs Sugiya with Nana and sister, Lina with Anna Maria Sheridan, Shelley with Sadie Goswell, Penny with Evie McCann, Kay with Ben Whiteley, Lynn with Esme Spencer, Carol with Hannah Tennant, Michelle with Charlie Terras, Nicki with Max Riggall, Tina with Lewis Oakey, Fiona with Ellie Messer, Sarah with Phoebe Berman
Hair and make-up: Tracy Townsend

Consultants

Warren Hyer MRCP is Consultant Paediatrician at Northwick Park and St. Mark's Hospitals, Harrow, and Honorary Clinical Senior Lecturer, Imperial College of Science, Technology and Medicine.
Penny Tassoni is an education consultant, author and trainer. Penny lectures on a range of childhood studies courses and has written five books, including *Planning, Play and the Early Years*.

Picture Credits

All other images © Dorling Kindersley. For further information see: www.dkimages.com
Picture librarian: Hayley Smith